# Newborn Care
# Training Workbook
# Foundational Program

## Newborn Care Specialist:
## A Nanny Specialized in Newborn Care

**Tonya Sakowicz**

# CONTENTS

Acknowledgments / Dedication     i

Module 1. What is a Newborn Care Specialist?     1

Module 2. The Newborn, Head to Toe     9

Module 3. Caring for the Newborn Baby     21

Module 4. Feeding, Medication and Diapering     29

Module 5. Building Your Nursery "Must-Have" List     36

Module 6. Special Needs of Preemies     43

Module 7. Building Up and Caring for a Postpartum Parent     47

Module 8. Caring for Multiples     53

Module 9. Reflux Symptoms and Management     63

Module 10. Tongue Tie and Lip Tie     69

Module 11. Pyloric Stenosis Signs and Symptoms     75

Module 12. Cleft Lip and Cleft Palate     79

Module 13. Food Allergies and Intolerances     83

Module 14. Swaddling Demonstrations     87

Module 14. To Swaddle or Not to Swaddle     95

Module 15. The Physiology of Sleep     99

Module 16. How Much Sleep Does a Baby Need & Patterns of Sleep     105

Module 17. Business, Legal, Taxes and Insurance     111

Module 18. Contract and Clients     116

Module 19. Working with and Educating Agencies     122

Module 20. Working with Clients that want to Go Green     125

Course Resources & Suggested Reading     127

Bibliography     130

Photo Attributions     135

About the Author     142

## Acknowledgement:

I would like to acknowledge some amazing people who have made this all possible. Without their help, this would still be just an idea.

First and foremost, my husband Todd. Without his vision, his business know-how, his willingness to take risks and most of all, his belief that we had something special here that could change the lives of babies and families through our students none of this would be real.

My amazing research assistant and test question writer, Danielle Bujnak. Those hours locked up together in my office with 3 computers between us have paid off!

Kellie Geres; hands down the best overall assistant anyone could ever ask for; Kellie kept so many balls in the air for us and we are so very grateful!

Jocelynn Yelverton; you asked and asked and asked, with your sweet southern charm and insistence and helped us make it happen. Thank you, my friend.

The Northwest Nanny Association; our test guinea pigs with the very first version of the live training "on-the-road". The nannies of the Pacific Northwest will always hold a special place in my heart.

Trisha Pffeifer with The Nanny Joynt in Phoenix--host of our very first run of this class ever!

And there is no thank you big enough for those who have walked this road of literally creating an industry with me:
Cortney Gibson, Lisa Williams, Clelie Bourne, Rowlanda Smith and so many others who were there they day we voted on the term Newborn Care Specialist and presented it to the International Nanny Association for consideration--LOOK what we have built!!!

And to the many others, both students and friends, who have stood alongside us, cheered us on, told others about our program and remind me daily why I do this, thank you! It is you we serve.


## Dedication:

This book is dedicated to all the wonderful families and countless babies over the years who have trusted me and taught me so much about what it is to come alongside new parents at the most vulnerable moment of their lives and help them grow into the wonderful families they were always meant to be; there is no greater teacher than experience. A special hug and dedication to the Weiss-Rife family and their triplets and big brother--your family is truly what allowed me to go from being a good caregiver to a specialist. I am forever grateful.

# Module 1

# What is a Newborn Care Specialist?

---

**Module 1. What is a Newborn Care Specialist?**

An introduction to the various types of caregivers who might be caring for newborns, and an in-depth discussion of the unique job description and personal qualities of the Newborn Care Specialist.

Notice these major ideas during this segment:

1. What are the differences between a Newborn Care Specialist and other caregivers who work with newborns?

2. What are the options for certification for Newborn Care Specialists in the U.S.?

**Recommended reading for this section:**

International Nanny Association: www.nanny.org

Childbirth and Postpartum Professional Association: www.CAPPA.net

DONA International: www.DONA.org

Newborn Care Solutions blog: https://newborncaresolutions.com/2016/03/17/big-buildings-and-strong-bridges-the-commModuley-we-all-belong-to/

# What is a Newborn Care Specialist (NCS)?

- Highly specialized and trained childcare provider who focuses on the care and well-being of the newborn
- Works independently with only minimal guidance from the parents
- Well versed in helping establish good feeding and sleeping habits
- Familiar with the behaviors, appearance and general care of the newborn
- Often has experience working with preemies and multiples
- Works hard to support a family's values
- Works hard to educate and build up the parents

Notes:

_____

_____

_____

_____

_____

_____

# What is a Newborn Care Specialist (NCS)?

- Keeps up on the latest information and studies in newborn care
- Is well versed in various sleep conditioning methods and has a successful plan for getting baby to sleep through the night and nap well
- Knows the limits of their scope of practice and follows them
- Hired predominantly to care for newborns for either overnight shifts or around the clock care
- Goals:
  - Healthy sleep patterns
  - Baby STTN as soon as reasonably possible
  - Healthy, empowered parent—usually identifies as a mother
- Understands the value of and can support breastfeeding parent

NEWBORN
CARE SOLUTIONS

Notes:

_____

_____

_____

_____

_____

_____

NEWBORN
CARE SOLUTIONS

# What is a Newborn Care Specialist (NCS)?

- ▸ Understanding of Postpartum Mood Disorders, can recognize them and confidently address the possibility when it arises
- ▸ Understanding of and can recognize signs of possible food allergies or intolerances and reflux; knows ways to help
- ▸ Behaves in a professional manner; maintaining family confidentiality
- ▸ Willing to share information with health care professionals in order to support optimal baby health
- ▸ Willing, at the appropriate time, to both be mentored and mentor others

Notes:

_____

_____

_____

_____

_____

_____

# What is a Night Nanny?

- A night nanny is just that—a nanny who works overnight shifts under the direct guidance and supervision of the parents
- May not have extensive training specifically in working with newborns,
- May not have extensive knowledge about sleep methodology
- May not recognize signs of Postpartum Mood Disorders, nor feel confident approaching parents about it
- May not recognize signs of reflux and food allergies/intolerances nor have any idea how to handle it
- Does not work independently
- Sometimes has some/all of the knowledge but does not use it (why?)

Notes:

_____

_____

_____

_____

_____

_____

# What is a Doula?

**Two Main Types**

- Labor Doula: educates and supports a pregnant mother before and during labor
- Postpartum Doula: helps provide support to the postpartum family in the first few weeks following birth through education, basic baby care, mother care and household assistance.  Her focus is on the entire family vs. primarily the newborn
- Other Doulas (bereavement, antepartum, abortion, adoption, others)
- All types have specific training and certification options through various training organizations
- Neither has a focus specifically on the newborn and sleep guidance for the new baby

NEWBORN
CARE SOLUTIONS

---

Notes:

_____

_____

_____

_____

_____

_____

NEWBORN
CARE SOLUTIONS

# What is a traditional nanny?

- A traditional nanny is a caregiver engaged by a family to care for children of many ages, although a nanny may specialize in a specific age group
- A traditional nanny works primarily days with occasional evenings, overnight or vacation care
- A traditional nanny may or may not have specialized training
- Around the world, traditional nannies may be categorized differently

Notes:

_____

_____

_____

_____

_____

_____

# Do I need to be certified to be an NCS?

- Certification can have some advantages
- Not required in the US and most Western Countries
- Various countries may have specific requirements
- Various Options within the US
- What makes a certification legitimate?
- INA (International Nanny Association) is currently adopting professional standards of practice, a Basic Skills Assessment, and a Credentialing Exam

Notes:

_____

_____

_____

_____

_____

_____

# Module 2

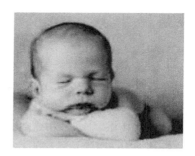

## The Newborn, Head to Toe

---

**Module 2. The Newborn, Head to Toe**

An investigation of conditions unique to the newborn age and stage of development, which can be encountered by a Newborn Care Specialist. Keep these questions in mind as you read about this stage of development:

1. What are the typical conditions and differences which can occur in newborns at or soon after birth?
2. What are some less common conditions and differences which can present in newborns up to several weeks after birth?

**Recommended reading for this section:**

Caring for your baby and young child by the AAP and Dr. Steven P Shelov
Caring for your newborn, how to enjoy the first 60 days by Dr. Olson Huff and Nicole Rawson-Huff
Having Your Baby, for the special needs of black mothers to be by by Dr. Hilda Hutcherson and Margaret Williams
The Flathead Syndrome Fix by Rachel Coley OT/L
Obstetrical Brachial Plexus Injuries by Rahul Nath, MD

# Newborns

- Often born with a waxy, cheese-like white substance called Vernix on their body— though usually only in term babies
- Often develops around 18 weeks gestation
- It is theorized to provide moisture and to facilitate passage through the birth canal; has antibacterial properties

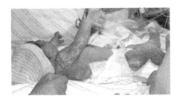 

Notes:

_____

_____

_____

_____

_____

_____

# Newborns

▷ Newborns are also often born covered in a fine layer of hair called Lanugo

▷ It is the first hair produced by fetal hair follicles and often appears around 5 months gestation

▷ It often disappears before birth, but in babies born with it, it falls out within a few days of birth in most instances

▷ Its purpose is to hold the Vernix on the skin so they are often seen together

Notes:

_____

_____

_____

_____

_____

_____

# The newborn head—appearance and care

- Newborn heads come in many shapes and sizes—they usually only come in the pretty round form in C-sections. They can be born with no hair, some hair, lots of hair.
- Babies hair does not need to be washed daily
- If baby has hair long enough to brush, use only a soft bristled brush

NEWBORN
CARE SOLUTIONS

---

Notes:

_____

_____

_____

_____

_____

NEWBORN
CARE SOLUTIONS

# Cradle cap

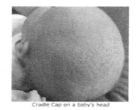
Cradle Cap on a baby's head

- Cradle cap is a common condition in newborns; most often presents as greasy skin covered by flaky white or yellow scales—occasionally with mild redness of the skin under it
- Often be the first sign of a food intolerance or allergy
- Cradle cap does not "need" to be treated, but parents often are highly disturbed by it
- Options include:
- Washing daily with a mild shampoo, using a gentle washcloth or baby brush to break up the scales
- Soaking babies scalp with olive or coconut oil for 15-30 minutes and then exfoliating
- More aggressive measures like dandruff shampoo are sometimes suggested by healthcare providers

NEWBORN
CARE SOLUTIONS

---

Notes:

_____

_____

_____

_____

_____

_____

NEWBORN
CARE SOLUTIONS

# Cradle cap or Eczema?

- Cradle Cap and Eczema have similar appearance—cradle cap is rarely itchy or uncomfortable—eczema is often itchy and uncomfortable
- The exact cause is not known, but most experts state:
- Hormones passed from the mother
- Yeast bacteria on the skin
- Food intolerances or allergies
- It is time to see the doctor when:
- Self care is not working
- The patches are interfering with babies eyes, nose or mouth
- The patches appear to be spreading, either in size or to new locations
- The parents are concerned

Notes:

_____

_____

_____

_____

_____

# The newborn head—facial appearance and care

- Wash babies face with warm water and a soft cloth—soap is not necessary in most instances
- Wash corners of eyes gently with soft cloth and water only as needed—the "gunk" in corners of the eyes is a normal part of eye cleaning itself. Never touch the eyeball
- Wash the outside of nose and nostrils with a soft cloth and water. Only use a nasal aspirator when needed for congestion—the nose is designed to flush itself. Saline can be used under the guidance of a healthcare professional
- Wash the inside of the mouth and gums with a soft cloth or baby "toothbrush" to help keep it clean
- Gently wash outside of ears with a soft cloth and water—do NOT put anything inside the ear canal
- Keep the neck area clean with a soft cloth and water—be sure to dry this area gently but well or a yeast infection can develop in skin folds

NEWBORN
CARE SOLUTIONS

Notes:

_____

_____

_____

_____

_____

_____

NEWBORN
CARE SOLUTIONS

# Concerns of the head and neck: Thrush

- Thrush-otherwise known as oral yeast infection. Often contracted by breastfeeding babies if the mother is on antibiotics. Can be passed back and forth between mother and baby.
- Requires careful washing and sterilizing of everything that comes in contact with both mother and baby
- Not dangerous, but requires medical assistance from a health  provider
- You do NOT diagnose—you suggest.
  Stay within the scope of your practice
- www.askdrsears.com

NEWBORN CARE SOLUTIONS

---

Notes:

_____

_____

_____

_____

_____

_____

NEWBORN CARE SOLUTIONS

# Concerns of the head and neck

- Torticollis means "twisted neck" in Latin and can happen because of positioning in the womb, difficult birth or sleep positioning
- It can be present at birth or show up in the first few weeks after birth and has a characteristic pulling of the head to one side, difficulty turning of the head, or even a preference to nurse on one side
- It can also present as a small knot or lump on the side of the neck
- It must be diagnosed by a doctor
- Can be helped sometimes by repositioning or simple stretches, but PT may be needed
- Babies with torticollis often can develop plagiocephaly
- You should never perform stretches without the direct guidance of a healthcare provider and a liability release from the parents
- Another big cause?

Notes:

_____

_____

_____

_____

_____

_____

# Concerns of the head and neck

▷ Desquamation: this is the peeling of the skin of a newborn—it is common and will usually resolve shortly after birth. A healthcare provider may suggest lotions to help

▷ Milia: small white bumps on the head and face that look like small whiteheads. In some cases they are even in the mouth. They go away on their own within a few days

▷ Newborn Acne: This is fairly common but may or may not go away on its own. Acne pustules should never be popped. Seek medical attention if it is of a concern

▷ Transient Pustular Melanosis: more common on darker skinned babies, it looks like Milia but often leaves a darker mark on the skin when it disappears

Notes:

_____

_____

_____

_____

_____

_____

# Brachial Plexus Injuries

- Injury to the Brachial Plexus, the bundle of nerves in the neck that provide signals to the arm and shoulder—sometimes even into the chest and leg
- Caused by the doctor pulling too hard on the babies head while twisting during delivery in most cases
- Babies with a brachial plexus injury often also have a broken clavicle due to shoulder dystocia
- Babies with a brachial plexus injury often have reflux and trouble sleeping because of nerve pain
- These babies require referral to a pediatric neurologist and brachial plexus specialist
- This injury can paralyze them for life, often requires extensive painful surgeries and years of Occupational Therapy
- If you are caring for a baby with a brachial plexus injury—call me

NEWBORN
CARE SOLUTIONS

Notes:

_____

_____

_____

_____

_____

_____

NEWBORN
CARE SOLUTIONS

# Characteristics of non-Caucasian babies

- Darker pigmentation of fingers and toes
- "Mongolian Spots" (slate gray nevi or congenital dermal melanocystosis) on back and extremities in many cases
- Note that Mongolian Spots can appear after birth an what this can mean for an NCS
- More purple-grey in color (Caucasian babies are usually red)
- Eyes are still often dark blue then change

Notes:

_____

_____

_____

_____

_____

_____

# Module 3.

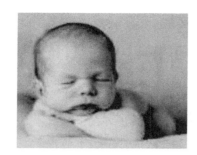

## Caring for the Newborn Baby

---

Module 3. Caring for the Newborn Baby

An overview of the routine care and feeding of the newborn infant which every Newborn Care Specialist should know. Reflect on these questions as you listen to the information in the segment:

1. What are common physical conditions and procedures which might affect the way you care for a newborn?

2. What is the NCS scope of practice in caring for and addressing potential issues in a newborn's physical health?

**Recommended reading & viewing for this section:**

http://www.abcdoula.com/shop/the-newborn-spa-bath-digital-download

Color Atlas & Synopsis of Pediatric Dermatology, Third Edition by Kay Shou-Mei Kane and Vinod E. Nambudiri

https://www.askdrsears.com/topics/health-concerns/skin-care/diaper-rash

# Caring for the Newborn Body

- Skin: warm water, mild soap and a soft wash cloth are all that is needed to clean the skin. Until the umbilical cord has healed (and circumcision if appropriate)*, clean using the "top and tail" method

- Be sure to dry baby well under the arms and in any skin folds to minimize risk of irritation and yeast infection development

- To take care of the umbilical cord, follow the instructions sent home with the parents—some healthcare professionals recommend rubbing alcohol, some recommend nothing except keeping it dry

- To take care of a circumcision, follow instructions sent home with parents—some healthcare professionals will recommend use of white petroleum jelly, others an antibiotic ointment, others nothing but gauze.

- Be aware of signs of infection in an umbilical cord or circumcision: redness, warmth, inflammation, oozing or puss. These require immediate medical attention

- Be aware of signs of adhesion with a circumcision: difficulty pulling the foreskin back, redness under edge of the foreskin after the circumcision has healed, little white "bumps" under the skin along circumcision edge

- A non-circumcised penis simply needs to be kept clean—there is no pulling of the foreskin required and damage can be caused to the penis by pulling on it

Notes:

_____

_____

_____

_____

_____

_____

# Caring for the Newborn Body

- Vaginal care for a newborn is much like any other female.  Always wipe front to back when changing a diaper, making sure to clean between the labial folds

- Do not put anything into the vaginal opening.  Do watch that the vaginal opening does not appear red or inflamed as this may be a sign of infection.  Also watch for closing of the vaginal opening—it is not common but does occur and requires the care of a medical professional---usually with a hormone cream

- The anus requires no special care unless there is sign of infection—a red ring around the anal opening can be an early sign of a food allergy (most often dairy) and red, scaling skin or weepy skin may indicate a strep infection.  These both require medical attention

Notes:

_____

_____

_____

_____

_____

# Newborn Genital appearance

Before

Normal healing    After

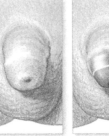
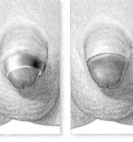

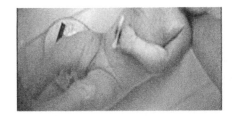

A.D.A.M.

NEWBORN
CARE SOLUTIONS

Notes:

_____

_____

_____

_____

_____

_____

NEWBORN
CARE SOLUTIONS

# Nails and Toes

▷ It is recommended that an NCS not trim babies nails for liability purposes. If it is too short, you cut the baby or they end up with an ingrown toenail, it falls on you as the responsible party

▷ Be aware of small threads and any hair that may get into the babies clothing, blankets or bed---babies seem to have a penchant for getting these wrapped around their toes and fingers creating a dangerous loss of circulation very quickly and could result in amputation

NEWBORN
CARE SOLUTIONS

Notes:

_____

_____

_____

_____

_____

_____

NEWBORN
CARE SOLUTIONS

# Diaper Rash, types and treatments

- Wet contact rash—just a redness or slight irritation of the skin—usually simple treatment with OTC diaper rash cream (or homemade—check online for recipes)
- Yeast—a raised, prickly red rash, usually starting in the folds of the skin. This requires medical attention and if cloth diapering, requires switching to disposables and treating cloth diapers once the rash is clear: http://theantijunecleaver.com/2013/01/how-to-remove-yeast-from-cloth-diapers/
- Acidic poop rash—looks and feels like a sunburn and can turn into burning open sores. Butt paste and sometimes antibiotic cream works well in most cases, but always seek medical advice
- Allergic rash—it could be from something in the diaper, detergent, environment or diet—this usually covers the entire diaper area and sometimes beyond. It requires medical attention, preferably from a pediatric allergist

Notes:

_____

_____

_____

_____

_____

_____

# Diaper Rash, types and treatments

- Impetigo—this is caused by staph or strep and appears as an open, weeping, crusty sore.  It requires medical treatment and is highly contagious

- Psoriasis—inflamed, scaly red patches of skin which can become infected.  This requires the attention of a dermatologists

- Eczema—red, itchy, scaly rash that can blister and weep—it looks much like cradle cap.  Be aware that this is often an early first sign of a food intolerance or allergy.  If mom is breastfeeding, a diet log is in order to try and identify associations with certain foods.  If formula feeding, a medical professional should be consulted about the possibility of a food allergy—most often a milk protein issue.

NEWBORN
CARE SOLUTIONS

Notes:

_____

_____

_____

_____

_____

_____

NEWBORN
CARE SOLUTIONS

# Bathing a baby

- Once the cord has dried and fallen off and the circumcision has healed, a baby may be given a full bath*
- Should ideally not be daily as it can dry out babies skin
- Warm water in an infant tub or lined sink, put a warm wet wash cloth or hand towel over exposed skin areas
- Bath from top to bottom
- Ideally bath at the same time daily (right before night time sleep is my preference to enhance sleep guidance) but all babies are different
- With medical approval, lavender oil in the bath water or massaged on baby following bath (in a carrier oil) can be extremely soothing and benefit sleep
- You can also (again with permission) diffuse lavender oil in the bathing area and/or nursery to enhance sleep

Notes:

_____

_____

_____

_____

_____

_____

# Module 4

## Feeding, Medication, and Diapering

---

**Module 4. Feeding, Medication and Diapering**

A general overview of what every Newborn Care Specialist should know when caring for a newborn baby. Your questions to consider as you go through this section:

1. Is there a simple answer to "Is breastmilk or formula the best?"

2. Why is a log so important when medication dispensing is part of your job?

**Recommended Reading for this section:**

Bestfeeding--how to breastfeed your baby by Mary Renfrew, Chloe Fisher and Suzanne Arms

The First Forty Days by Heng Ou

Your Baby and Child by Dr. Penelope Leach

The Nursing Mother's Companion by Kathleen Huggins

# Feeding a newborn

- The Age Old Debate—breast or bottle. We all know that "breast is best," or do we?
- In most cases, breastfeeding is the healthiest option for the baby, assuming mom is relatively healthy, both physically and mentally
- Bottle feeding breast milk is the next healthiest option
- Bottle feeding formula or specialized formula is the least healthy option
- Why is breast sometimes not the best?
- When mom has a medical condition that makes it hard or impossible for her to breastfeed (thyroid disease, pituitary disease, PCOS, medication that passes through the breast milk that is dangerous to baby)
- When mom is struggling emotionally postpartum and it is just "one more thing" that adds stress to her life
- When baby has a medical condition (rare) that makes breastfeeding incompatible-called Galactosemia and makes baby unable to digest sugars. It requires specialized formulas and immediate medical attention

Notes:

_____

_____

_____

_____

_____

_____

# Feeding a newborn

So, if breastfeeding, does mom's diet matter?

- Many foods/chemicals pass through breastmilk
- We don't know all of them that do or do not
- Blind studies say that it doesn't matter
- Moms and experience tell us differently and we know moms diet can produce gas, constipation, diaper rash and more in the newborn baby. Mom can also pass potential allergens through to baby (cows milk protein intolerance, etc..) and can be a major contributor to an unhappy baby and disturbed sleep
- Ideally we like to see a non-GMO, organic and balanced diet heavy in most fruits and veggies, lean healthy protein and healthy fats and minimally processed grains. Avoiding most processed foods is highly beneficial and most babies do better when mom avoids dairy, particularly uncooked dairy

NEWBORN
CARE SOLUTIONS

---

Notes:

_____

_____

_____

_____

_____

_____

NEWBORN
CARE SOLUTIONS

# Feeding a newborn

- Formula Feeding—what are the options and what is healthiest?
  - Conventionally made dairy and soy based formulas
  - Organic dairy and soy based formulas
  - Goats Milk/Goats Milk- Hipp and Holle Baby are the most common—otherwise recipes online (caution)
  - Online recipes for other homemade formula options (caution)
- Never be the one to tell mom what she should do—always phrase it, "Perhaps it would be a good idea to talk to your pediatrician about the possibility of considering...." You are not a medical professional and it is outside your scope of practice

Notes:

_____

_____

_____

_____

_____

_____

# Medications and the Newborn

- Never dispense medication of any kind to a baby in your care without specific instructions from the parents and the child's healthcare provider and a medical liability release. You never want to assume responsibility for a medical decision.

- We are providing a sample form for you—it is recommended that you clear the use of this form on the advice of an attorney

- Always double and triple check medication dispensing information and keep a written log of any medications administered and the dosage

- Insist parents also keep track in the written log so that everyone is on the same page

Notes:

# Diapering a newborn

▷ Cloth vs Disposable—which is better?

▷ Cloth is considered better by most because over time there is less environmental damage and a smaller carbon footprint from cloth diapers, particularly now with HE washers. Cloth diapers also tend to have less diaper rash because of less chemical exposure and more frequent changing

▷ Cloth at night can lead to more wakefulness at night in sensitive babies so diaper doublers are helpful

▷ Disposable is more convenient for sure, but has a greater environmental impact both in the production and disposal

▷ Easier for travel and overnights

▷ If disposable is chosen, then go with a healthier option; there are many available these days and www.mamanatural.com has a great review of many brands

Notes:

_____

_____

_____

_____

_____

_____

# What about wipes?

- Most baby wipes are loaded with chemical cleaners; not great for using in the genital area and directly on the skin—we absorb toxins through our skin
- Safest is a soft cloth, water and gentle soap
- Safer brands do exist and www.safemama.com has a great review of some of these
- You can also find a variety of green 'recipes' online for making your own baby wipes utilizing a variety of products including essential oils

NEWBORN
CARE SOLUTIONS

Notes:

_____

_____

_____

_____

_____

_____

NEWBORN
CARE SOLUTIONS

# Module 5

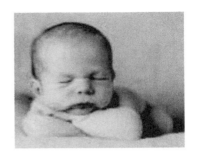

# Building your Nursery "must have" List

---

**Module 5. Building your nursery "must-have" list**

This list can be gold for you and your clients.  In this section, we will talk about the items often needed (and not needed) in the typical nursery and why we use some of them, as well as some guidelines for keeping things clean.  As you go through this section, keep in mind the following:

1.  What things are truly necessary in a nursery?

2.  What things need special cleaning consideration and why?

**Recommended Reading for this section:**

Raising Baby Green by Dr. Alan Greene

Green Baby by Susannah Marriott and Dr. Lawrence Rosen

http://articles.extension.org/pages/25770/cleaning-sanitizing-and-disinfecting-in-child-care

# Building your nursery "must have" list

- For each NCS and each client, this list will vary a little
- As you gain experience with certain products, you will develop a preference
- Some NCS require specific name brands; be careful
- Some families will have way more, some will balk at your list
- You decide how critical each item is through time and experience.
- Just because a client has twins or triplets, not everything on the list has to double or triple
- Some things are absolutes such as a safe and proper sleeping situation and properly installed safe car seats

Notes:

_____

_____

_____

_____

_____

# Building your nursery "must have" list

- Proper car seat, installation checked by a CPST (what is this?)
- Crib or bassinet that meets current AAP safety guidelines
- Swaddle blankets (3 or more)
- Crib sheets (3)
- Onesies (3)
- Sleepers or nightgowns (3)
- Diapers (2 packs newborn, 1 Costco case size 1-2) or 20 cloth with covers
- Baby wipes
- Changing table area (this can be the top of a dresser or inside a wardrobe type cabinet) with pad and 2-3 covers and storage
- Mini crock pot or bottle warmer

Notes:

_____

_____

_____

_____

_____

_____

# Building your nursery "must have" list

- Thermometer
- Nasal aspirator
- Saline solution
- Diaper rash cream
- Sound machine that does not have an automatic shut-off
- Pacifiers (if using)
- Breast pump if planning to breast feed—ideally hospital grade, along with proper tubing, collection bottles, etc...
- At least 4 bottles with stage 1 nipples
- 3-5 daytime outfits
- Moby wrap or other front carrier
- Breastfeeding pillow, properly fit to your body type

Notes:

_____

_____

_____

_____

_____

_____

# Building your nursery "must have" list

- Trash can and liners
- Diaper pail
- Green nursery cleaner
- Nail clippers
- Anti-gas drops
- Baby bath tub and bath wash (preferably organic)
- Wash cloths and towels (4,2)
- Baby hair brush or comb
- Bottle brush
- Nipple basket or sterilizer
- Bottle drying rack or pad
- Burp cloths (6)

NEWBORN
CARE SOLUTIONS

---

Notes:

_____

_____

_____

_____

_____

_____

NEWBORN
CARE SOLUTIONS

# Building your nursery "must have" list

- Dirty laundry hamper
- Laundry soap (free and clear or green laundry soap)
- Laundry stain remover
- Clean clothes hamper or basket
- Stroller
- Pack and play (optional)
- Diaper bag or backpack
- Baby monitor
- Rocking chair and table
- Baby hangers if using closet for clothing

Notes:

_____

_____

_____

_____

_____

# Building your nursery "must have" list

- Facial Tissue
- Room darkening "black out" shades
- Motion monitor (Babysense, Owlet, etc…)
- Ceiling or floor fan
- Playmat
- Soft toys
- Board books with bright and contrasting colors
- Swing or bouncy seat
- Dimmable night light or switch added to lamp
- Nursery clock (low light)

Notes:

_____

_____

_____

_____

_____

_____

# Module 6

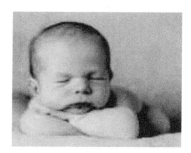

## Special Needs of Preemies

---

Module 6. Special Needs of Preemies

As Newborn Care Specialists, we are often brought in to assist with Premature infants. Understanding the everyday basics and different needs of premature infants can help you manage this special circumstance. Keep these questions in mind through this section:

1. Do premature infants have different nervous system responses vs. term infants?

2. Premature infants sleep more than term infants—why?

**Recommended Reading for this section:**

Your Premature Baby and Child by Amy E. Tracy

Parenting Your Premature Baby and Child, the Emotional Journey by Debra L Davis and Mara Tesler Stein

The Premature Baby Book by Dr. William Sears and Robert Sears

# Special Needs of Preemies

- One of my favorite books: Your Premature Baby and Child
- Depending on size, they may need specialized car seats. The Car Seat Lady has a comprehensive list on her website at http://thecarseatlady.com/tips-for-preemies/
- They need smaller clothing
- Preemie sized diapers if using disposables
- May come home on a variety of monitors or with special medical devices—be sure that you attend any training with the parents to ensure you know how to properly use them.
- May need specialized high calorie formula—familiarize yourself with it and how to mix it properly
- Very likely will have reflux (90% of preemies do)
- Their nervous system is not as developed—they are much more sensitive to touch, light, smell and sudden or loud sounds
- They don't eat much
- They sleep more than term babies
- They are more vulnerable to illness and RSV in particular

NEWBORN
CARE SOLUTIONS

---

Notes:

_____

_____

_____

_____

_____

_____

NEWBORN
CARE SOLUTIONS

# Special Needs of Preemies

- Their skin is very thin and scratches/tears easily
- Preemies often struggle with wakefulness because their primary need is growth (babies grow when asleep)
- Preemies also often struggle with feeding—their sucking reflex is not yet fully developed
- Preemies may "appear" to have sleep issues because they are so very tired and do not yet have night and day rhythms. They have different patterns.
- Preemies have reflux in the majority of cases, usually requiring medical intervention of some kind because of the lower esophageal sphincter not being fully developed
- Preemies often later have sight development issues
- Preemies are usually later to reach milestones in the first year to 18 months of life. Usually by 18 months to 2 years they have caught up to term babies
- Parent(s) may be more likely to have PPMD—be aware

Notes:

_____

_____

_____

_____

_____

_____

# Swaddling a preemie baby

▷ Preemies have specific definitions

▷ Late preterm: 34-36 weeks

▷ Moderately preterm: 32-34 weeks

▷ Very premature: 25-32 weeks

▷ Extremely premature: at or before 25 weeks

▷ They should be swaddled with arms up before 37 weeks, so either swaddle with arms up or use a swaddle designed specifically for this purpose (and this is just a guideline)

▷ The arms up is the natural position they hold most in utero and since they were born early, it helps with proper development of the arms and shoulders and with feeding cues/alertness until at least 37 weeks. If arms still feel "stiff" or "tight" then continue to swaddle with arms up until you feel the arms naturally soften and not resist when gently brought to babies side

Notes:

_____

_____

_____

_____

_____

_____

# Module 7

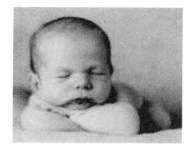

## Building Up and Caring for a Postpartum Parent

NEWBORN
CARE SOLUTIONS

---

### Module 7. Building Up and Caring for a Postpartum Parent*

The postpartum period can be highly challenging for new parents, and these challenges are not just limited to birth mothers. In this segment we will consider these questions in mind through this section:

1. How do we encourage and build up a postpartum parent?

2. How do we bring up concerns about a potential problem?

3. What are the main symptoms we might see in a parent struggling with a postpartum mood disorder?

**Recommended Reading for this section:**

Postpartum Mood and Anxiety Disorders, A Clinician's Guide Beck, Cheryl Tatano, Driscoll, Jeanne Watson

Identifying Perinatal Depression and Anxiety: Evidence-based Practice in Screening, Psychosocial Assessment and Management 1st Edition by Jeannette Milgrom

The Pregnancy and Postpartum Anxiety Workbook: Practical Skills to Help You Overcome Anxiety, Worry, Panic Attacks, Obsessions, and Compulsions by Pamela S. Wiegartz, Kevin L. Gyoerkoe, Laura J. Miller

*We use both the terms "parent" and "mom" in this section; most NCS clients identify as mothers or as mom.

# Caring for and building up a postpartum mom

- Understand that it is the most important job you have besides keeping baby safe
- Understand that she doesn't even understand her emotions or her body right now
- Understand that her reactions to you are not personal
- Understand that she may be experiencing jealousy
- Understand that she is SCARED
- While the baby is your primary responsibility, your goal is a healthy, empowered mom, so help ensure she gets proper:
  - Rest
  - Hydration
  - Nutrition
  - Breaks
  - Healthcare
  - Assurance
  - Psychological support if needed

Notes:

_____

_____

_____

_____

_____

_____

# Caring for and building up a postpartum mom

- ▷ Encourage her efforts, not point out her mistakes or take over
- ▷ Be patient with her
- ▷ Don't criticize; let her make mistakes and learn from them
- ▷ Listen to her fears if she wants to talk—she's new to this
- ▷ Remind her she is important to her baby and family and to take care of herself
- ▷ Be sure if you see signs of a PPMD you notify her partner if she has one and help her seek professional assistance
- ▷ Be supportive of her choices—this is her baby not yours
- ▷ If she has had a C-section, encourage her to follow doctors advice for healing
- ▷ Be reasonably flexible—she may change her mind...often

☺

Notes:

_____

_____

_____

_____

_____

_____

## PPMD: Baby Blues, Postpartum Depression, Postpartum Anxiety and Postpartum Psychosis

- Postpartum hormones are insane and scary
- What are "baby blues" vs true PPD?
  - BB is exhaustion, anxiety, tears, fears, mild depression and moodiness; up to 80% of new moms experience it. It can last up to a few weeks but decreases over time and goes away
  - PPD is similar symptoms, (or no feelings at all) but more severe, often increases in intensity, even to the point of disconnection from the baby or suicidal thoughts and instead of going away, lingers and often worsens
  - Postpartum Anxiety is more characterized by a racing mind, restlessness, a need to be "doing something" all the time, worried all the time, scary, disturbing thoughts, compulsive need to check things and more
  - PP Psychosis is a rare but severe form of PPD which also includes confusion, delusions, thoughts of harming their baby, hallucinations, refusal to eat or sleep, etc.
  - Baby blues are usually handled without medical intervention, PPD and PPP require medical intervention
  - Great resource: http://www.postpartumprogress.com/the-symptoms-of-postpartum-depression-anxiety-in-plain-mama-english

NEWBORN
CARE SOLUTIONS

Notes:

_____

_____

_____

_____

_____

_____

NEWBORN
CARE SOLUTIONS

## How do I bring up my concerns about Postpartum Mood Disorder?

- Bring it up before you are contracted—in the initial discussion
- Bring it up again when you arrive for your first shift
- Make sure mother's partner knows you will come to them with concerns
- When you address it up front in a matter of fact way, you help reduce the stigma many feel over it and help them know you care and don't judge.  If you have seen it before, without sharing client info, share that:
  - "I have had clients experience it before and getting proper help quickly made it so much better for their family"
- Have a prepared "speech" for bringing it up:
  - "I have seen some signs that may indicate what 'Mary' is experiencing is more than simple Baby Blues.  Because of the following signs (be specific—she's not eating, she doesn't seem to want to care for junior, she hasn't showered in 5 days in spite of plenty of opportunities, she is sleeping more than the baby, etc.) I am very concerned for her mental health.  It is my recommendation you contact her healthcare provider right away for help in determining if this is just Baby Blues or if it is something more serious."

Notes:

_____

_____

_____

_____

_____

_____

# Helping support a breastfeeding mom

- Encourage and praise her efforts without being pushy
- Learn all you can about breastfeeding
- DO NOT give advice if you are not trained in this area, even if you are an experienced breastfeeder yourself
- Encourage her to seek the help of a LC if she is having issues or pain
- Be sure she is getting adequate rest, nutrition and is hydrating well
- Bring baby to her and then step back but stay close
- Support her if she decides that breastfeeding is not for her

Notes:

_____

_____

_____

_____

_____

_____

# Module 8

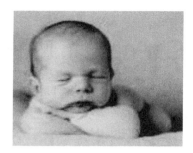

## Caring for Multiples

NEWBORN
CARE SOLUTIONS

---

<u>**Module 8. Caring for Multiples**</u>

Multiples can be quite a challenge, but certain protocols can make life easier. This segment will review various options to make life with multiples easier for families. Questions to consider:

1. Will scheduling make life with multiples easier in most cases?

2. What are some special considerations for multiples when feeding?

**Recommended Reading for this section:**

Mothering Multiples: Breastfeeding and Caring for Twins or More! (La Leche League International Book) by Karen Kerkhoff Gromada

Twins 101: 50 Must-Have Tips for Pregnancy through Early Childhood From Doctor M.O.M.

Healthy Sleep Habits, Happy Twins by Dr. Marc Weissbluth

Mothering Multiples: Breastfeeding and Caring for Twins or More! (La Leche League International book) by Karen Kerkhoff Gromada

Twins 101: 50 Must-Have Tips for Pregnancy through Early Childhood from Doctor M.O.M. by Khanh-Van Le-Bucklin, MD

# Caring for Multiples

- Many times an NCS is brought in because a family is expecting multiples
- There are unique challenges and great solutions to caring for more than one baby at a time

Notes:

_____

_____

_____

_____

_____

_____

# Scheduling for Multiples

- Get babies and parents used to a schedule as soon as possible—they won't always have an extra set of hands
- Begin by writing it out and sharing
- Remember/remind parents that it will change as babies get older; this is temporary
- Decide with parents what they want (all at once, one at a time)
- My recommendations:
  - All babies wake at the same time, eat at the same time, bath at the same time
  - This may mean waking a baby up for a feeding or to keep to the schedule
  - Ultimately this will mean for greater sanity for family when you are gone

Notes:

_____

_____

_____

_____

_____

_____

# Planning for a Multiples Homecoming

- ▷ Have the refrigerator well stocked so parents don't need to go out for groceries or eat take out every day
- ▷ Have everything stocked so you don't have to go to store for at least 2 weeks for baby supplies or know delivery options
- ▷ Have the nursery set for all babies coming home at once
- ▷ Plan for both situations anyway (important to discuss)
- ▷ If only one comes home at a time, expect that to effect parental emotions
- ▷ Be prepared to be flexible as parents may have to go back and forth to the hospital for other babies
- ▷ Be prepared for strong emotions if there are siblings
- ▷ Have your scheduling plan ready to go

Notes:

_____

_____

_____

_____

_____

_____

# Vehicles and Car Seats

- Be sure to discuss this in advance with clients, particularly if triplets or more as special car beds or car seats may need to be obtained
- Have contact with a local CPST who can advise parents on choosing the proper car seats and helping parents learn to install them
- Our company expert: Lisa Cote  carseatsafetynut@gmail.com
- NEVER, NEVER, NEVER install a car seat for your clients or tell them their install looks great—refer them to a CPST
- If you are using your car to transport, have the parent install the seat in your vehicle and ensure you have proper insurance coverage
- If you want to be able to install and teach parents, become at certified CPST
- Want to be a tech?  cert.safekids.org

NEWBORN
CARE SOLUTIONS

Notes:

_____

_____

_____

_____

_____

NEWBORN
CARE SOLUTIONS

# Sleep for Multiples

- Probably one of the most critical elements for family sanity
- Scheduling is key
- Sleeping through the night as soon as reasonably possible
- Good sleep habits during the day
- Critical to discuss this with the family in advance of the babies arrival or your start date
- Everyone needs to be on the same page
- If there are extra hands (grandparents, volunteers, etc.) develop a written plan and ask parents to ensure EVERYONE follows it
- "Rock" one baby at a time

Notes:

_____

_____

_____

_____

_____

# Feeding Multiples

- Different methods for feeding all at once; find yours
  http://multiples.about.com/od/twinfants/ss/Feeding-Twins.htm
- Be well-prepared in advance
- Be sure all caregivers are following the same plan
- Be prepared to be flexible
- Have a labeling system (colors, tags, etc.)
- If babies are on different formulas or medications, be extra cautious

Notes:

_____

_____

_____

_____

_____

# Feeding Multiples

Devices for feeding multiples:

- Pacifeeder
- Podee
- Bebe bottle sling
- Bottle snuggler
- Bottle Genie

NEWBORN
CARE SOLUTIONS

Notes:

_____

_____

_____

_____

_____

_____

NEWBORN
CARE SOLUTIONS

# Everybody is crying!

- It IS going to happen; it doesn't mean you are doing anything wrong or are failing
- Discuss this with the parents in advance—explain it will happen to them and it will happen to you
- Assess the situation and see whose need is greatest
- Food or sleep comes before a wet diaper
- Illness trumps food or sleep
- Address the greatest need and then move on to the next
- Keep yourself calm; if you get stressed, the babies will know it and it will up their stress level and stress response
- Know when to ask for help

Notes:

_____

_____

_____

_____

_____

_____

# Recognizing Signs of Various Feeding Issues

- We will look more closely at how feeding affects scheduling and sleep, but first, signs of feeding issues:
- Reflux:

**Symptoms of Reflux:**
- Acidy smelling bowel movements
- Frequent Spitting Up and/or Regurgitation
- Frequent Choking Episodes
- Unexplainable cough not related to a cold
- Fighting the feeds
- Unexplainable crying (often diagnosed as colic)
- Irritability
- Not content, always moving
- Frequent Upper Respiratory colds
- Chronic or Frequent Ear Infections
- Vomiting Frequently (more than normal "spit-up")

Notes:

_____

_____

_____

_____

_____

_____

# Module 9

# Reflux Symptoms and Management

---

Module 9. Reflux Symptoms and Management

Understanding the signs of reflux and how to assist in symptom management is key to a Newborn Care Specialist. In this section, consider and be able to:

1. identify the common signs of reflux
2. Have a clear understanding of the most common treatments

**Recommended Reading for this section:**

Colic Solved by Dr. Brian Vartabedian

Acid Reflux in Infants and Children by Tracey Davenport and Mike Davenport

https://www.mayoclinic.org/diseases-conditions/infant-acid-reflux/symptoms-causes/syc-20351408
https://medlineplus.gov/refluxininfants.html

# Reflux...

- Hiccups
- Appear hungry & 'attack' the bottle/breast and then pull away after a few drinks crying
- Arching of the neck and back
- Bad breath or Sour breath
- Sticking fingers or fist into the back of the throat (may be a sign of Esophagitis
- Gagging themselves (may be a sign of Esophagitis)
- Hoarse Voice
- Full feeling belly
- Excessive gas
- Wheezy breathing sound
- Gargling noise
- Baby may have poor weight gain
- Baby may eat a lot more or want to suck more often
- Failure to thrive or losing weight
- Nasal congestion
- Heartburn
- Indigestion
- Apnea spells

> A baby may have some of these symptoms, all of these symptoms, or only 1 or 2. Still if you suspect reflux consult a medical doctor. Reflux is most often misdiagnosed as colic or other illnesses.

NEWBORN
CARE SOLUTIONS

Notes:

_____

_____

_____

_____

_____

_____

NEWBORN
CARE SOLUTIONS

# How to help relieve reflux

▷ Keep the baby upright for about 30-45 minutes after a feeding. You can use a bouncy chair, swing, hold or wear baby or put them in a boppy type pillow.

▷ Avoid laying the child flat. For sleeping try elevating the head of the crib to a 30 degree angle (see nest instructions); or try using a Tucker Sling or Baby Stay Asleep.

▷ Create a reflux "nest" in the crib to support the child on the elevated surface*
  ▷ Take a large bath towel and roll in into a cylinder lengthwise. Then fold it into a "U" shape.
  ▷ Place on top of the crib mattress, but under the sheet, with the bottom of the "U" where the baby's bottom will rest with his legs going over the top of the bump from the towel.
  ▷ The ends of the towel come up on either side of the baby to prevent them from rolling.
  ▷ They should come no higher than the baby's armpit to avoid a baby getting their face stuck against the towel and smothering.

▷ **Use of a reflux nest requires a liability release**

Change feeding schedule to give the child smaller meals more frequently if possible.

Notes:

# How to help relieve reflux

- Refluxers often reflux less when sleeping on their tummy versus their back.
- However, this can increase the risk of SIDS and families should always contact their doctor before trying it.
- **In addition, obtain a liability release from the client if they wish to tummy sleep**
- Avoid tight clothing especially around the belly.
- Avoid holding the baby in such a way as to put pressure on the belly.
- Some doctors recommend thickening the feeds with cereal or trying a thicker formula such as Enfamil AR (designed for refluxers). The starting recommendation is rice cereal and 1 teaspoon per ounce. Start slow and work up as it is harder to suck thick formula and you don't want to frustrate baby. There are now special nipples made that are silicone and cut in a "Y" shape that make feeding rice thickened formula easier. If the rice is too constipating I suggest Oatmeal. It is high in fiber and helps even things out. I also recommend premixing your cereal bottles. The cereal absorbs better and thickens evenly. Do not do this without consulting your pediatrician first.

Notes:

_____

_____

_____

_____

_____

_____

# How to help relieve reflux

- Switching to Playtex or Dr. Brown's bottles, as both do more than others to prevent air from getting into the baby's tummy, which seems to aggravate the gag reflex for those reflux babies that spit up or projectile vomit.

- If the family is using formula, consider switching to a non DHA/ARA formula, as the ARA can often irritate the stomach (ARA can cause inflammation of the stomach lining and intestinal tract) of a reflux baby and make the reflux worse. These are not easy formulas to find, but more of the organic ones are carrying it this way. Again, do not do this without discussing it with the pediatrician first.

- Soy formula or hypo-allergenic (Alimentum, Neocate, etc.) formulas can also be a great help, but soy is not recommended except as a last resort. Reflux and food allergies seem to be a common combination and this is why these options often help. If a baby needs the hypo-allergenic formulas, with a note from the doctor, families can sometimes get their insurance company to cover the cost—They may have to fight for it, but it does get sometimes get covered.

NEWBORN
CARE SOLUTIONS

Notes:

_____

_____

_____

_____

_____

NEWBORN
CARE SOLUTIONS

# More reflux information

- ▶ Because reflux can be difficult to manage and scary for parents, it helps if you know about some of the tests and treatments
- ▶ Tests: Most often it is treated without tests, but severe cases may have tests run
  - ▶ Upper GI Barium Swallow
  - ▶ PH Probe
  - ▶ Edoscopy, sometimes with biopsy
- ▶ Treatments:
  - ▶ Zantac (Ranitidine).  You want it compounded if at all possible
  - ▶ Axid (Nizatidine)
  - ▶ Prevacid (Lansoprazole)
  - ▶ Prilosec (Omeprazole)
  - ▶ Antihistamines like Benadryl
  - ▶ Reglan (Metoclopramide)

Notes:

_____

_____

_____

_____

_____

_____

# Module 10

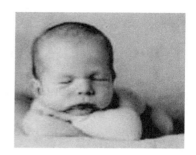

## Tongue Tie and Lip Tie

---

### Module 10. Tongue Tie and Lip Tie

This segment is to familiarize you with the basic symptoms and understanding of tongue tie and lip tie as Newborn Care Specialists are often the ones to encounter and potentially recognize tongue and lip tie in the newborn.

Questions for considering during the segment:

    1. What is tongue tie?

    2. What are the main symptoms of tongue tie?

    3. What is lip tie?

**Recommended Reading for this section:**

TONGUE TIE Morphogenesis, Impact, Assessment and Treatment. Alison K. Hazelbaker

https://tonguetie.net/breastfeeding/

http://www.llli.org/Illleaderweb/lv/lvaprmay02p27.html

# Tongue Tie and Lip Tie

- Tongue tie—abnormal attachment of the lingual frenulum that can interfere with a proper latch and impede breastfeeding and speech

- Lip tie—abnormal attachment of the upper frenulum that impedes movement of the upper lip

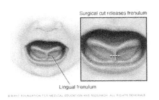  

NEWBORN
CARE SOLUTIONS

Notes:

_____

_____

_____

_____

_____

NEWBORN
CARE SOLUTIONS

# Signs of tongue or lip tie

▶ Tongue tie is sometimes not "visible" but still exists; sometimes it may just be the tongue appears shorter or that the whole floor of the mouth raises with the tongue movements

  ▶ Signs of an issue in mom:
  • nipple pain and/or erosions
  • nipple looks pinched, creased, bruised or abraded after feeds
  • white stripe at the end of the nipple
  • painful breasts/vasospasm
  • low milk supply
  • plugged ducts
  • mastitis
  • recurring thrush
  • frustration, disappointment, and discouragement with breastfeeding
  • weaning before mom is ready

Notes:

_____

_____

_____

_____

_____

_____

# Signs of tongue or lip tie

▶ Signs in baby:
- poor latch and suck
- unusually strong suck due to baby using excess vacuum to remove milk
- clicking sound while nursing (poor suction)
- ineffective milk transfer
- infrequent swallowing after initial let-down
- inadequate weight gain or weight loss
- irritability or colic
- gas and reflux
- fussiness and frequent arching away from the breast
- fatigue within one to two minutes of beginning to nurse
- difficulty establishing suction to maintain a deep grasp on the breast
- breast tissue sliding in and out of baby's mouth while feeding
- gradual sliding off the breast
- chewing or biting on the nipple
- falling asleep at the breast without taking in a full feed
- coughing, choking, gulping or squeaking when feeding
- spilling milk during feeds
- jaw quivering after or between feeds

Notes:

_____

_____

_____

_____

_____

_____

# Assessing for possible tongue tie

▸ **Assessing baby for tongue-tie: (baby may not have every sign)**
- **Does baby's tongue rise less than half-way to the palate when crying?**
- **Do the sides of the tongue lift but not the center?**
- **Can you see a dip in the tongue in the center of the mouth?**
- **Does tongue have a heart shaped tip?**
- **Does baby have a high, narrow or bubble palate?**
- **Can you see or feel a tight frenulum?**

▸ To feel for a restrictive frenulum, you can use the "Murphy Maneuver," developed by San-Diego pediatrician Dr. James Murphy. Use medical grade gloves (non-latex) Put your little finger at the base of baby's tongue and draw across the floor of the mouth. If you feel a resistance in the center of baby's mouth, that is the frenulum. If you cannot get past this frenulum without going around it, then it may be restrictive enough to affect baby's ability to breastfeed

▸ You are not the doctor, however, and must refer the parents on to their healthcare provider with your suspicions, not your "diagnosis"

Notes:

_____

_____

_____

_____

_____

# To clip or not to clip

▷ Like most trends in childcare, it comes and goes

▷ Current tide is swinging back towards not to clip

▷ It is a personal decision between the family and their healthcare provider

▷ Dr. Agarwal at Agave Pediatrics in Scottsdale, AZ is considered an expert in this here in the US, as is Dr. Gaheri in Portland, OR.  There are others around the world as well.

▷ www.agavepediatrics.com

Notes:

_____

_____

_____

_____

_____

_____

# Module 11

## Pyloric Stenosis Signs and Symptoms

---

Module 11. Pyloric Stenosis Signs and Symptoms

This segment is designed to help you have a clear understanding of the most common symptoms of this rare but serious newborn infant medical condition.

Questions to keep in mind during this segment include:

1. What happens within the stomach that results in a diagnosis of pyloric stenosis?

2. Pyloric Stenosis is more common in what racial population?

3. Can pyloric stenosis symptoms wait for the next pediatric appointment?

**Recommended Reading for this section:**

https://www.mayoclinic.org/diseases-conditions/pyloric-stenosis/symptoms-causes/syc-20351416

https://emedicine.medscape.com/article/929829-overview

https://jamanetwork.com/journals/jama/fullarticle/186078

# Pyloric Stenosis – signs and treatment

- Narrowing or restriction (stenosis) of the pylorus, the muscular lower part of the stomach.
- Prevents food from properly emptying into the intestines
- Usually shows up between 3-5 weeks post birth
- Genetic component
- More common in first born males
- More common in Caucasian babies than others
- Use of the antibiotic Erythromycin by the mother late in pregnancy, while breastfeeding or in the baby during the first weeks of life is a factor

Before    After

✦ADAM.

NEWBORN
CARE SOLUTIONS

---

Notes:

NEWBORN
CARE SOLUTIONS

# Signs of pyloric stenosis

- ▷ Vomiting—seems like spit up at first but becomes projectile, in an arc from the mouth and can go several feet, usually soon after eating
- ▷ It may be curdled from stomach acid, but will not contain bile (greenish thick liquid)
- ▷ Babies have fewer, smaller, sometimes mucousy stools because little food is actually reaching the intestine
- ▷ Babies will fail to gain weight, become lethargic and possibly dehydrated from lack of food
- ▷ Waves of peristalsis, or left to right rippling or waves of movement across the babies abdomen as the stomach tries to empty itself after feeding

NEWBORN
CARE SOLUTIONS

Notes:

_____

_____

_____

_____

_____

NEWBORN
CARE SOLUTIONS

# Treatment of pyloric stenosis

- Immediate referral to a healthcare provider
- Proper logging of feeds/reactions will help diagnose quicker
- Ultrasound of babies stomach/intestines (it can be seen!)
- Barium swallow
- Blood test for salt imbalance from dehydration
- Pyloromyotomy—muscles are cut around and relaxed to allow the food to pass into the intestines properly
- Most babies can begin to feed normally within a few hours post surgery

Notes:

_____

_____

_____

_____

_____

# Module 12

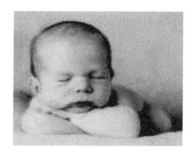

# Cleft Lip and Cleft Palate

---

## Module 12. Cleft Lip and Cleft Palate

This segment is designed to give you a basic understanding of the conditions of cleft lift and cleft palate. It is recommended that if you are working with a child with this condition that you have specific training from the healthcare providers directing care rather than second-hand from a parent or other caregiver.

Questions to keep in mind during this segment include:

1.  What is the difference between a cleft lip and a cleft palate?

2.  Can you have both a cleft lip and a cleft palate at the same time?

**Recommended Reading for this section:**

Evaluation and Management of Cleft Lip and Palate by David J. Sajac and Linda Vallino

Cleft Lip and Palate: Diagnosis and Management by Samuel Berkowitz

https://www.healthychildren.org/English/health-issues/conditions/Cleft-Craniofacial/Pages/Cleft-Lip-and-Palate-Parent-FAQs.aspx

http://www.cleftline.org/who-we-are/what-we-do/publications/for-the-parents-of-newborn-babies-with-cleft-lipcleft-palate/

# Cleft lip and cleft palate

▶**Cleft lip** and **palate** are birth defects that happen while a **baby** is developing in the uterus . During the 6th to 10th week of pregnancy, the bones and tissues of a baby's upper jaw, nose, and mouth normally come together (fuse) to form the roof of the mouth and the upper lip.  An interruption of this process can cause cleft lip or palate

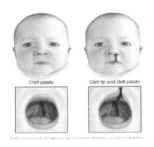

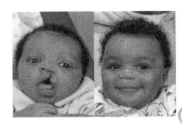

NEWBORN
CARE SOLUTIONS

---

Notes:

_____

_____

_____

_____

_____

_____

NEWBORN
CARE SOLUTIONS

# Feeding a baby with cleft lip or palate

**Breastfeeding**

▷ Breastfeeding an infant with a cleft lip but no cleft palate can be successful, but sometimes requires a changed feeding position so that mother's breast tissue fills the gap in the lip or gum.

▷ Breastfeeding an infant with a cleft palate is quite challenging unless the infant's cleft palate is very far in the back of the mouth and very small. Nursing at the breast is best limited to 10 minute sessions, and supplemental bottles will be needed if breastfeeding alone does not supply enough food for adequate satisfaction and growth.

▷ For most mothers of infants with cleft palate, breast pumping should begin in the birth hospital using a high quality electric breast pump and continue after each infant feeding.

▷ A lactation consultant is a breastfeeding mother's best resource for correct positioning and pumping technique. Discuss your feeding plan with this specialist before discharge from the hospital.

Notes:

_____

_____

_____

_____

_____

# Feeding a baby with cleft lip or palate

**Bottle feeding**

- Small, frequent feedings
- Semi upright feeding position to limit milk going into nasal passage
- Head, neck and shoulders in straight line or tilted forward (not back)
- Pull lower jaw down and out of the way if needed to get nipple in properly
- Watch for signs of distress (no breathing in 3-4 sucks, squirming, etc.) and remove bottle, calm baby and begin again
- Use specialized bottle systems such as a cleft palate nurser, pigeon nipple or Haberman

Notes:

_____

_____

_____

_____

_____

# Module 13

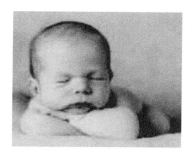

## Food Allergies and Intolerances

---

<u>**Module 13. Food Allergies and Intolerances**</u>

This segment is designed to familiarize you with the major allergens effecting children and how they may present.

Things to consider:

1. What is the main difference between an intolerance and allergic response?

2. What is the most common allergen in infants?

**Recommended Reading for this section:**

Dietary Management of Food Allergies and Intolerances by Janice Vickerstoff Joneja, PhD

Dealing with Food Allergies in Babies and Children by Janice Vikerstoff Joneja, PhD

The Breastfeeding Mama's Guide to an Allergy-free Diet www.mightymoms.club

Food Allergies: A Complete Guide for Eating When Your Life Depends on it by Scott H. Sicherer

# Food Allergies and Intolerances

▶ Earliest signs can be seen within just a couple weeks of birth, but most don't appear until around 6 weeks—the same time as reflux

▶ Cradle cap

▶ Acne

▶ Red ring around anal opening

▶ Hives or rash

▶ Vomiting after eating

▶ Loose, acidic stools (can even "burn" the skin)

▶ Cramping and pain following a feeding

▶ Crying, often about an hour post feeding

▶ Blood or mucous in the stools

▶ Anaphylaxis—swelling of mouth or tongue and inability to breath

Notes:

_____

_____

_____

_____

_____

_____

# What's the difference between an allergy and intolerance?

- ▷ Intolerance causes discomfort and some physical symptoms
- ▷ A true allergy produces a histamine response either intestinally, externally (hives, rash) or anaphylactic (swelling, difficulty breathing, loss of consciousness)
- ▷ This must be evaluated by a proper healthcare provider—often times a standard pediatrician does not recognize the signs and many signs mimic those of reflux (which often goes hand in hand)
- ▷ Pediatric allergy specialist
- ▷ Treatment can include:
- ▷ Avoidance of foods by mother if breastfeeding or specialty formulas if bottle feeding
- ▷ Administering an antihistamine if needed, epi pen, auvi-q

Notes:

_____

_____

_____

_____

_____

_____

# The "Big 8" allergens

**The Big-8**

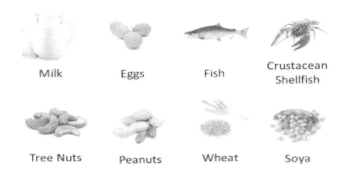

| Milk | Eggs | Fish | Crustacean Shellfish |
| --- | --- | --- | --- |
| Tree Nuts | Peanuts | Wheat | Soya |

Notes:

_____

_____

_____

_____

_____

_____

# Module 14

Please Note:

The next several pages contain step by step photos for you reference of the live baby
swaddling demonstrations shown in our Swaddling Demos chapter of this program.

The PowerPoint notes resume on page 95 of this workbook.

Swaddling (step by step)

## Swaddling (step by step)

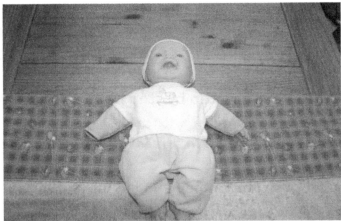

NEWBORN
CARE SOLUTIONS

Notes:

_____

_____

_____

_____

_____

_____

NEWBORN
CARE SOLUTIONS

# Swaddling (step by step)

NEWBORN
CARE SOLUTIONS

Notes:

_____

_____

_____

_____

_____

_____

NEWBORN
CARE SOLUTIONS

# Swaddling (step by step)

Notes:

_____

_____

_____

_____

_____

_____

## Swaddling (step by step)

Notes:

_____

_____

_____

_____

_____

Swaddling (step by step)

Notes:

_____

_____

_____

_____

_____

_____

## Swaddling (step by step)

# Swaddling with a Miracle Blanket
www.miracleblanket.com

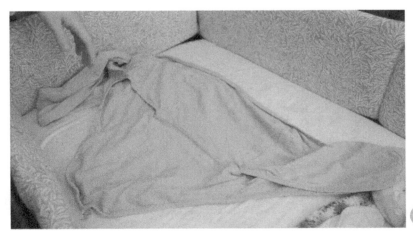

# Module 14

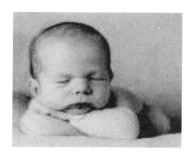

## To Swaddle or Not to Swaddle

NEWBORN
CARE SOLUTIONS

---

**Module 14. To Swaddle or Not to Swaddle**

This segment is designed to give you information on the pros and cons of swaddling and to give you the current recommendations on swaddling from around the world.

Questions to keep in mind:

1. What is the purpose of swaddling a newborn baby?

2. Are there any dangers associated with swaddling?

3. How do we prevent swaddling associated hip dysplasia issues?

**Recommended Reading for this section:**

The Happiest Baby on the Block by Dr. Harvey Karp

Secrets of the Baby Whisperer by Tracy Hogg

The Origins, Prevention and Treatment of Infant Crying and Sleep Problems by Ian St. James-Roberts

http://www.7swaddles.com/all-videos/

# To swaddle or not to swaddle?

- Huge controversy, particularly in the last couple years
- As of now, the AAP still recommends swaddling as a safe practice following their specific guidelines:
  - Back to sleep
  - When to stop
  - Know the risks
  - Keep the hip area looser—baby should be able to bend hips up and out
  - Follow AAP basic guidelines for safe sleep
    - Back to sleep
    - No loose blankets
    - Crib free of bumpers, soft bedding, wedges, toys, pillows and positioners
    - Crib or bassinet, not the parents bed
    - Avoid overheating
    - Use a pacifier
    - Smoke free area

Notes:

_____

_____

_____

_____

_____

## Swaddle Options

- Miracle blanket
- Aden and Anais Muslin
- Swaddle Me
- Woombie
- Sleep sacks with swaddle flaps
- Love to Dream Swaddle Up (for arms up swaddling)
- Swaddle Pod
- Comfort and Harmony Peanut Swaddle
- Choose based on what you and the parents are most comfortable with and the size/needs of the baby

NEWBORN
CARE SOLUTIONS

Notes:

_____

_____

_____

_____

_____

_____

NEWBORN
CARE SOLUTIONS

# Swaddling Mistakes

- #1, not swaddling tight enough.

- #2, swaddling with the arms up near the face or bent. No matter how tightly you swaddle, if you leave the arms bent or up near babies face, they will break the swaddle. Now, one important note: if a baby is born before 37 weeks, it is best to try to swaddle them with their arms bent

- #3, making assumptions about how the baby 'feels' about swaddling based on adult feelings. Yes, you and I would likely hate to be tightly wrapped each night, but the reality is that most babies love to be in tight spaces (why they often snuggle up to bumpers)

- #4, allowing the blanket to touch the cheek.

- #5, allowing the end of the swaddle blanket to come loose. Many cultures even tie their babies into a swaddle to ensure this does not happen.

**NEWBORN** CARE SOLUTIONS

Notes:

_____

_____

_____

_____

_____

**NEWBORN** CARE SOLUTIONS

# Module 15

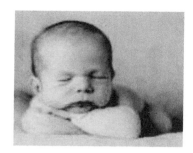

# The Physiology of Sleep

---

## Module 15. The Physiology of Sleep

This segment is designed to give you a better understanding of the physiology of sleep including sleep cycle lengths in infants, and a clear understanding of the safe sleep environment. For this segment, you will need to be able to understand:

1. What is the difference between REM and non-REM sleep?

2. What makes a sleep environment safe or unsafe?

3. Understanding the basics of various popular sleep methods

**Recommended Reading for this section**

The Happiest Baby on the Block by Dr. Harvey Karp
12 Hours Sleep by 12 Weeks Old by Suzy Giordano
The Self-Calmed Baby by William A.H. Sammons
Secrets of The Baby Whisperer by Tracy Hogg
Healthy Sleep Habits, Happy Baby by Dr. Marc Weissbluth
Sleeping Through the Night by Jodi A Mindell, PhD
Solve Your Child's Sleep Problems by Dr. Richard Ferber
On Becoming BabyWise by Gary Ezzo and Robert Buckham

# The Physiology of Sleep

- 2 main types of sleep—REM and non REM

- Non REM sleep is what we most closely associate with sleep, meaning that there is very little movement during this time, our breathing and heart rate is slow and steady, and there is very little, if any dreaming during this stage. During REM sleep, the body is much more active and this is when we actually dream. Although both are necessary, it is believed that most of our restorative sleep comes during the non REM stage.

- During non REM sleep, there are 4 distinct phases that we go through as we progress from being drowsy to deep sleep. Stage 1 is the drowsy, drifting off stage and the stages progress all the way to a stage 4 where only very specific types of things (such as a child screaming in fear) would wake you and yet you may still awaken feeling a bit disoriented.

Notes:

_____

_____

_____

_____

_____

# Sleep

▶ Sleep cycle length

  ▶ 45 mins for a baby, 90 minutes for an adult
  ▶ We transition to adult circadian rhythm around age 3
  ▶ REM sleep begins to develop at approx. 6 months gestation
  ▶ Non-REM around 7 months gestation
  ▶ Babies brain development and sleep patterns are different
  ▶ "Adult" thinking does not apply to babies

Notes:

_____

_____

_____

_____

_____

- Back to Sleep Campaign 50-80% drop in SIDS
- Around 2005, the AAP determined that side sleeping is also not safe
- Modern crib (coke can test)
- No loose blankets
- No bumpers
- No stuffed animals
- No pillows
- No layered quilts
- No co-sleeping (AAP recommendation; different than room sharing)

Notes:

_____

_____

_____

_____

_____

_____

# Sleep training-major methods

- The Happiest Baby on the Block—Dr. Harvey Karp
- 12 Hours Sleep by 12 Weeks Old
- The Self-Calmed Baby
- Secrets of the Baby Whisperer
- Healthy Sleep Habits, Happy Baby—Dr. Marc Weissbluth
- Sleeping Through the Night—Dr. Jodi Mindell
- Solve Your Childs Sleep Problems—Dr. Richard Ferber
- On Becoming Babywise—Gary Ezzo and Dr. Robert Bucknam
- Other options

Notes:

_____

_____

_____

_____

_____

# My methods 😊

▶ A combination of the "best practices" of all the major methods combined with years of working with the best teachers (babies!)

▶ So why is every job the "same" and yet "different"?
  ▶ Proper feeding, especially during the day
  ▶ Proper scheduling based on age
  ▶ Paying attention to sleep cues
  ▶ Proper steps
  ▶ Proper environment
    ▶ Dark room
    ▶ No TV or screen time
    ▶ Swaddling
    ▶ White noise
    ▶ Fan
    ▶ Crib or bassinet in child's own room

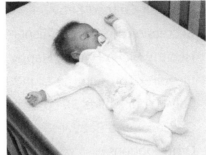

Notes:

_____

_____

_____

_____

_____

# Module 16

## How Much Sleep Does a Baby Need and Patterns of Sleep

---

### Module 16. How Much Sleep Does a Baby Need and Patterns of Sleep

This segment is designed to give you a basic understanding of how many hours of sleep per day you can expect from a baby in your care and what normal sleep patterns look like, keeping in mind of course, that each baby is different, and needs will vary.

Your questions to consider in this segment are:

1.  Do sleep needs change as a "neuro-typical" baby gets older and how do they change?

2.  Do most babies follow a fairly standard pattern of sleep development?

3.  Are there outside factors that may affect normal baby sleep and what are they?


**Recommended Reading for this section**:

Healthy Sleep Habits, Happy Child by Dr. Marc Weissbluth

Sleeping Through the Night by Jodi A. Mindell, PhD

The Happiest Baby Guide to Great Sleep by Dr. Harvey Karp

Solve Your Child's Sleep Problems by Dr. Richard Ferber

# So how much sleep does a baby need?

▶ **For a newborn:** 16-22 hours per day (note: a newly circumcised baby boy may sleep for an extended period, possibly up to 12 hours immediately following the procedure)

▶ **3-6 months:** 15-18 hours per day

▶ **6-12 months:** 14-16 hours per day

▶ **12-18 months:** 14-15 hours per day

▶ **18-24 months:** 13-15 hours per day

Notes:

_____

_____

_____

_____

_____

_____

# Patterns of Sleep

**Birth to 4 months:**

- Sleep will be random, but will start to work itself into a pattern of waking in the AM and going back down for a nap 1-2 hours after waking.

- Sleeping for 1½-3 hours, then waking again for 1-2 hours, and back down for an afternoon nap

- Waking again, up for 1-2 hours, another nap

- Up again for another 1-2 hours and then into bed for the night, with possible wakings depending on age and size

Notes:

# Patterns of Sleep

**Between 4 and 6 months:**

▶ Most babies are capable of sleeping at least an 8-hour stretch at night and many can sleep up to 12 hours

▶ Provided the baby is at least 12 lbs., they have no physiological need to eat at night (unless there is a health problem), although I have often found that some little girls seem to need to double their birth weight in order to sleep through

▶ They also move into a daytime pattern at this age of waking, an AM nap about 2 hours later, waking, an afternoon nap about 2 hours later, waking, a short late afternoon nap about 1-2 hours later, waking after an hour, then back down for the night 1-2 hours later.

Notes:

_____

_____

_____

_____

_____

_____

# Patterns of Sleep

▶ **Somewhere between 6 and 9 months,** most babies will drop that late afternoon nap and move to a schedule of one morning nap and one afternoon nap and should easily be sleeping 11-12 hours at night

▶ This pattern will likely continue until **somewhere between 15-18 months,** when the AM nap is often dropped and baby can stay awake 4-5 hours between sleep periods

▶ **Usually by 18 months,** most babies are only one nap per day and will stay that way up until 2½-3 years of age or longer

Notes:

_____

_____

_____

_____

_____

_____

## Problems you may encounter with sleep — what do you do?

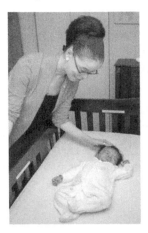

- ▶ Baby may have health issues
    - ▶ Reflux
    - ▶ Allergies
    - ▶ Failure to thrive
    - ▶ Pyloric stenosis
- ▶ Parents may not be following through but think they are
- ▶ Parents may change their minds
- ▶ Baby may be more sensitive
- ▶ Baby may have undiagnosed (and undetectable) issues
    - ▶ Autism
    - ▶ Sensory Integration Disorder

NEWBORN
CARE SOLUTIONS

---

Notes:

_____

_____

_____

_____

_____

NEWBORN
CARE SOLUTIONS

# Module 17

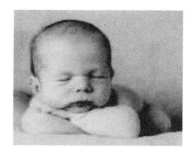

## Business, Legal, Taxes and Insurance

---

**Module 17. Business, Legal, Taxes and Insurance**

An overview of the concerns that affect your business as an NCS, which will vary based on your residential location as well as your work location.

Questions to consider include:

1. How could consulting with a qualified attorney assist me in developing an effective contract and other business documents?

2. How could consulting with a qualified tax professional assist me in understanding and meeting my tax obligations, without paying any extra taxes that are not required?

**Recommended Reading for this section:**

Government Tax and Insurance Requirements for your personal State, Province and Country as this will vary from region to region and country to country.

# Getting your NCS Business Going!

What is first?

- ▶ Training and Mentorship
- ▶ Develop your "elevator speech"
- ▶ Build your references/gain experience
- ▶ Resume/Portfolio
- ▶ Website with good head shot
- ▶ Domain specific email (tonya@newborncaresolutions.com)
- ▶ FB page
- ▶ Market Yourself via print advertising, google ads, offering free classes/speaking for moms groups
- ▶ Start a blog
- ▶ Have a phone script

Notes:

_____

_____

_____

_____

_____

_____

# Are there any legal issues?

- You will want to have a contract that clearly outlines what you provide, for how long, for what rate, with what expectations of the client, your fee payment structure, grounds for you ending the contract, refund policies
- Liability releases for administering of medications, parents asking you to follow non AAP recommended guidelines, special considerations like medical conditions and monitors
- Understanding that most states are "at-will" work states and how that affects any contract you have with a client; and LLC can help some
- Really should consider consulting an attorney
- You are a mandated reporter in most cases
- Understand the laws in your area; states and countries vary

Notes:

_____

_____

_____

_____

_____

_____

# Are there any tax issues?

- Am I an independent contractor?
- Can I be paid with a company check?
- Does my client have to get an EIN?
- What if my client wants to 1099 me?
- What if my client wants to pay me cash?
- Should I get professional tax help?
- Am I paid under my name or my business name?

Notes:

_____

_____

_____

_____

_____

# What about insurance?

- Do I need insurance?
  - Pros and Cons
- What kind?
  - Liability
  - Malpractice
- Where do I find it?
  - Talk to an insurance agent that represents businesses
  - Contact insurers who insure doulas

Notes:

_____

_____

_____

_____

_____

_____

# Module 18

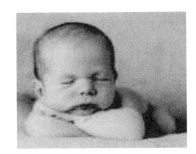

## Contracts and Clients

---

**Module 18. Contracts and Clients**

In this section we will explore the NCS contract; what it should cover, why those areas need to be covered and how to work with your client to have a contract that is fair and agreeable to both parties.

# Contracts? Do I need one and what goes on it?

Do I need one?

- ▸ Yes, in most cases
- ▸ When you can opt not to worry about it
- ▸ Why do I want one?
- ▸ What if a client doesn't want to use one?

Notes:

_____

_____

_____

_____

_____

# So what goes in a contract?

- Period of Contract
- Termination of Contract by either party
  - Non compliance of parents with agreed upon plan
  - Change of plan
  - Inappropriate treatment of NCS
  - Inappropriate behavior of NCS
  - Loss of Pregnancy
  - Change of Plans
- Amendments to the Contract
- Responsibilities Outlined
- Planned Work Schedule

Notes:

_____

_____

_____

_____

_____

# What goes in a contract?

- Monetary Considerations
  - Hourly rate
  - Unused services
  - Deposit
  - Total contract compensation
  - Taxes
- Accommodations within the home for NCS
- Food provision for the NCS
- Use/respect of clients home including private spaces
- List of supplies client agrees to provide by the first day of work
- Goals of the client and NCS
- Use of cameras within the home

Notes:

_____

_____

_____

_____

_____

# How do I get paid?

- ► Terms outlined in the contract
- ► Deposit, remainder paid via schedule
- ► Cash, Check, Paypal, Square and other card readers
- ► They forgot!
- ► The check bounced!
- ► They are refusing to pay me per our contract!

Notes:

_____

_____

_____

_____

_____

# I have a potential client on the phone —now what?

- Have a prepared script based on your elevator speech
- Have a "nugget" to give away that shows you are knowledgeable
- Don't give away the farm
- Know what you offer—I don't offer 24 hour care because I don't do it. Be clear with yourself on what you will and won't do
- Limit your phone conversation time "I would love to share with you what services I can offer your family—I have 5 minutes right now or we can set up a 15 min appt later today"
- If you like to and have the time, offer to meet in person, but limit the time—protect your knowledge
- Refer them to your website where they can "see" you and what you offer

Notes:

_____

_____

_____

_____

_____

# Module 19

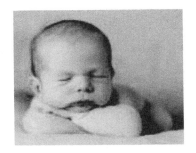

## Working with and Educating Agencies

---

Module 19.  Working with and Educating Agencies

**Working with and Educating Agencies**

In this section, we will explore ways to share with agencies about what a Newborn Care Specialist is, what an NCS offers to families and how you can work together with the agency to promote placement of Newborn Care Specialists, increasing job opportunities for you and revenue for the agency.

# Working with and educating agencies

- Call local agencies who you would like to place you and offer to take their placement person out for coffee
- Explain what you do that is different than a "night nanny" and ask if they do placements
- Offer to help them put together a script that they can use with potential clients
- Encourage them to share your services even with a family who is looking to hire a nanny—they can earn more fees by placing an NCS and then a nanny
- Encourage them to offer a "package" deal for families that do both

Notes:

_____

_____

_____

_____

_____

_____

# Are there NCS specific agencies?

- Yes, but only a few in the US. There may be more in other countries but they may use different terminology and have different practices.
- Be sure you know what they need from you
- Be sure you know how you are getting paid and that it is legal
- Be sure there is still a contract between you and the family

Notes:

_____

_____

_____

_____

_____

# Module 20

## Working with Clients that want to Go Green

NEWBORN
CARE SOLUTIONS

---

<u>Module 20. Working with Clients that want to Go Green:</u>

This segment is designed to give you the basics of what you need to know in order to assist your client families who wish to lead a greener lifestyle.

The following questions should be kept in mind as you review the content:

1   What is one free and simple way to improve the environment and reduce toxins inside the home?

2   Why are the kitchen, bathroom and laundry room often the most toxic rooms in the home?

**Recommended Reading for this section:**

Green Body, Green Birth by Mary Oscategui

Healing the New Childhood Epidemics: Autism, ADHD, Asthma and Allergies by Kenneth Bock

Green Babies, Sage Moms: The Ultimate Guide to Raising Your Organic Baby by Linda Fossa

# So my clients say they want to go green?

- Air quality, both inside and outside the home
- Creating a healthy nursery and bedroom
- Products we use in our hair and on our bodies (for us and our client babies)
- Creating and maintaining healthy play areas
- Cleaning in the Kitchen
- What we eat
- How we clean the bathroom
- What is used in the laundry room
- In the car
- Off to school

Notes:

_____

_____

_____

_____

_____

_____

# Course Resources:

Bestfeeding--how to breastfeed your baby by Mary Renfrew, Chloe Fisher and Suzanne Arms
The First Forty Days by Heng Ou
Your Baby and Child by Dr. Penelope Leach
The Nursing Mother's Companion by Kathleen Huggins
http://www.kellymom.com
http://www.llli.org
http://www.who.int/nutrition/topics/infantfeeding_recommendation/en/


Raising Baby Green by Dr. Alan Greene
Green Baby by Susannah Marriott and Dr. Lawrence Rosen
http://articles.extension.org/pages/25770/cleaning-sanitizing-and-disinfecting-in-child-care
Green Body, Green Birth by Mary Oscategui

Your Premature Baby and Child by Amy E. Tracy
Parenting Your Premature Baby and Child, the Emotional Journey by Debra L Davis and Mara Tesler Stein
The Premature Baby Book by Dr. William Sears and Robert Sears

Postpartum Mood and Anxiety Disorders, A Clinician's Guide Beck, Cheryl Tatano, Driscoll, Jeanne Watson

Identifying Perinatal Depression and Anxiety: Evidence-based Practice in Screening, Psychosocial Assessment and Management 1st Edition by Jeannette Milgrom

The Pregnancy and Postpartum Anxiety Workbook: Practical Skills to Help You Overcome Anxiety, Worry, Panic Attacks, Obsessions, and Compulsions by Pamela S. Wiegartz, Kevin L. Gyoerkoe, Laura J. Miller


Mothering Multiples: Breastfeeding and Caring for Twins or More! (La Leche League International Book) by Karen Kerkhoff Gromada
Twins 101: 50 Must-Have Tips for Pregnancy through Early Childhood From Doctor M.O.M. Khanh-Van Le-Bucklin, MD
Healthy Sleep Habits, Happy Twins by Dr. Marc Weissbluth

Colic Solved by Dr. Brian Vartabedian
Acid Reflux in Infants and Children by Tracey Davenport and Mike Davenport
https://www.mayoclinic.org/diseases-conditions/infant-acid-reflux/symptoms-causes/syc-20351408
https://medlineplus.gov/refluxininfants.html

TONGUE TIE Morphogenesis, Impact, Assessment and Treatment. Alison K. Hazelbaker
https://tonguetie.net/breastfeeding/

http://www.llli.org/Illeaderweb/lv/lvaprmay02p27.html

https://www.mayoclinic.org/diseases-conditions/pyloric-stenosis/symptoms-causes/syc-20351416
https://emedicine.medscape.com/article/929829-overview
https://jamanetwork.com/journals/jama/fullarticle/186078

Evaluation and Management of Cleft Lip and Palate by David J. Sajac and Linda Vallino
Cleft Lip and Palate: Diagnosis and Management by Samuel Berkowitz
https://www.healthychildren.org/English/health-issues/conditions/Cleft-Craniofacial/Pages/Cleft-Lip-and-Palate-Parent-FAQs.aspx
http://www.cleftline.org/who-we-are/what-we-do/publications/for-the-parents-of-newborn-babies-with-cleft-lipcleft-palate/

Dietary Management of Food Allergies and Intolerances by Janice Vickerstoff Joneja, PhD
Dealing with Food Allergies in Babies and Children by Janice Vikerstoff Joneja, PhD
The Breastfeeding Mama's Guide to an Allergy-free Diet  www.mightymoms.club
Food Allergies: A Complete Guide for Eating When Your Life Depends on it by Scott H. Sicherer

The Happiest Baby on the Block by Dr. Harvey Karp
12 Hours Sleep by 12 Weeks Old by Suzy Giordano
The Self-Calmed Baby by William A.H. Sammons
Secrets of The Baby Whisperer by Tracy Hogg
Healthy Sleep Habits, Happy Baby by Dr. Marc Weissbluth
Sleeping Through the Night by Jodi A Mindell, PhD
Solve Your Child's Sleep Problems by Dr. Richard Ferber
On Becoming BabyWise by Gary Ezzo and Robert Buckham
https://www.ncbi.nlm.nih.gov/pmc/articles/PMC2724135/
https://www.aap.org/en-us/about-the-aap/aap-press-room/pages/american-academy-of-pediatrics-announces-new-safe-sleep-recommendations-to-protect-against-sids.aspx

The Happiest Baby on the Block by Dr. Harvey Karp
Secrets of the Baby Whisperer by Tracy Hogg
The Origins, Prevention and Treatment of Infant Crying and Sleep Problems by Ian St. James-Roberts

Healthy Sleep Habits, Happy Child by Dr. Marc Weissbluth
Sleeping Through the Night by Jodi A. Mindell, PhD
The Happiest Baby Guide to Great Sleep by Dr. Harvey Karp

Solve Your Child's Sleep Problems by Dr. Richard Ferber

Green Body, Green Birth by Mary Oscategui
Healing the New Childhood Epidemics: Autism, ADHD, Asthma and Allergies by Kenneth Bock
Green Babies, Sage Moms: The Ultimate Guide to Raising Your Organic Baby by Linda Fossa

# *Bibliography of Recommended Readings*

**Unit 1:**

International Nanny Association: www.nanny.org

Childbirth and Postpartum Professional Association: www.CAPPA.net

DONA International: www.DONA.org

"Big Buildings & Strong Bridges: the community we ALL belong to" https://newborncaresolutions.com/2016/03/17/big-buildings-and-strong-bridges-the-community-we-all-belong-to/

**Unit 2:**

Shelov, S. P. (Ed.), (2015). *Your baby's first year* (4th ed.). New York, NY: Bantam Books.

Huff, O. & Rawson-Huff, N. (2009). *Caring for your newborn: how to enjoy the first 60 days as a new mom.* Asheville, NC: Sixty-Second Parent.

Hutcherson, H. & Williams, M. (1997). *Having your baby: for the special needs of black mothers to be, from conception to newborn care.* New York, NY: One World.

Coley, R. (2015). *The flathead syndrome fix: a parent's guide to simple and urprising strategies for preventing plagiocephaly and rounding out baby's flat spots without a helmet.* Charlotte, NC: CanDo Kiddo.

Nath, R. (2006). *Obstetrical brachial plexus injuries.* College Station, TX: virtualbookworm.com.

**Unit 3:**

Newborn Spa Bath http://www.abcdoula.com/shop/the-newborn-spa-bath-digital-download

Kane, K. S., Nambudiri, V. E. & Stratigos, A. J. (2016). *Color atlas & synopsis of pediatric dermatology.* (3rd ed.). New York, NY: McGraw-Hill Education.

Diaper Rash https://www.askdrsears.com/topics/health-concerns/skin-care/diaper-rash

**Unit 4:**

Renfrew M., Fisher, C. & Arms, S. (2004). *Bestfeeding: how to breastfeed your baby.* Berkeley, CA: Celestial Arts.

Ou, H. (2016). *The first forty days.* New York, NY: Stewart, Tabori & Chang.

Leach, P. (2010). *Your baby and child.* New York, NY: Knopf.

Huggins, K. (2007). *The nursing mother's companion.* (6th ed.). Beverly, MA: Harvard Commons Press.

# *Bibliography of Recommended Readings*

**Unit 5:**

Greene, A. (2007). *Raising baby green: the earth-friendly guide to pregnancy, childbirth and baby care*. Hoboken, NJ: Jossey-Bass.

Marriott, S. & Rosen, L. (2008). *Green baby*. New York, NY: DK Publishing.

Cleaning, Sanitizing & Disinfecting in Child Care articles.extension.org/pages/25770/cleaning-sanitizing-and-disinfecting-in-child-care

**Unit 6:**

Tracy, A. E. (1999). *Your premature baby and child*. New York, NY: Berkley Trade.

Davis, D. L. & Stein, M.T. (2004). *Parenting your premature baby and child: the emotional journey*. Golden, CO: Fulcrum Publishing.

Sears, W. & Sears, R. (2004). *The premature baby book*. New York, NY: Little, Brown & Co.

**Unit 7:**

Beck, C. T. & Driscoll, J. W. (2005). *Postpartum mood and anxiety disorders: a clinician's guide*. Burlington, MA: Jones & Bartlett Learning.

Milgrom, J. & Gemmill, A. (Eds.). (2015). *Identifying perinatal depression and anxiety: evidence-based practice in screening, psychosocial assessment and management*. (1st ed.). West Sussex, U.K.: John Wiley & Sons, Ltd.

Gyoerkoe, K. L., Miller, L. J. & Wiegartz, P. S. (2009). *The pregnancy and postpartum anxiety workbook: practical skills to help you overcome anxiety, worry, panic attacks, obsessions, and compulsions*. Oakland, CA: New Harbinger.

**Unit 8:**

Gromada, K. K. (2007). *Mothering multiples: breastfeeding and caring for twins or more!* (3rd ed.). Franklin Park, IL: La Leche League International.

Le-Bucklin, K. (2008). *Twins 101: 50 must-have tips for pregnancy through early childhood from doctor M.O.M.* Hoboken, NJ: Jossey-Bass.

Weissbluth, M. (2009). *Healthy sleep habits, happy twins*. New York, NY: Ballantine Books.

**Unit 9:**

Vartabedian, B. (2007). *Colic solved: the essential guide to infant reflux and the care of your crying, difficult-to-soothe baby*. New York, NY: Ballantine Books.

Davenport, T. & Davenport, M. (2007). *Acid reflux in infants and children*. Centreville, MD: SportWork.

# Bibliography of Recommended Readings

The Mayo Clinic "Infant Reflux" https://www.mayoclinic.org/diseases-conditions/infant-acid-reflux/symptoms-causes/syc-20351408

MedLine "Reflux in Infants" https://medlineplus.gov/refluxininfants.html

**Unit 10:**

Hazelbaker, A. K. (2010). *Tongue tie morphogenesis, impact, assessment and treatment.* Columbus, OH: Aidan and Eva Press.

Breastfeeding with Tongue Tie https://tonguetie.net/breastfeeding/

Tongue Tie & Breastfeeding www.llli.org/llleaderweb/lv/lvaprmay02p27.html

**Unit 11:**

The Mayo Clinic "Pyloric Stenosis" https://www.mayoclinic.org/diseases-conditions/pyloric-stenosis/symptoms-causes/syc-20351416

Pediatric Hypertrophic Pyloric Stenosis https://emedicine.medscape.com/article/929829-overview

Familial Aggregation & Heritability of Pyloric Stenosis https://jamanetwork.com/journals/jama/fullarticle/186078

**Unit 12:**

Zajac, D. J. & Vallino, L. (2015). *Evaluation and management of cleft lip and palate.* Plymouth, U.K.: Plural Publishing.

Berkowitz, S. (Ed.). (2013). *Cleft lip and palate: diagnosis and management.* New York, NY: Springer.

Caring for babies with cleft lip and/or palate https://www.healthychildren.org/English/health-issues/conditions/Cleft-Craniofacial/Pages/Cleft-Lip-and-Palate-Parent-FAQs.aspx

For the parents of newborn babies with cleft lip/cleft palate http://www.cleftline.org/who-we-are/what-we-do/publications/for-the-parents-of-newborn-babies-with-cleft-lipcleft-palate/

**Unit 13:**

Joneja, J. V. (1998). *Dietary management of food allergies and intolerances.* New York, NY: J A Hall Publications.

Joneja, J. V. (2007). *Dealing with food allergies in babies and children.* Boulder, CO: Bull Publishing Co.

The Breastfeeding Mama's Guide to an Allergy-Free Diet https://www.mightymoms.club/breastfeeding-allergy-free-diet/

# Bibliography of Recommended Readings

Sicherer, S. H. (2017). *Food allergies: a complete guide for eating when your life depends on it.* (2nd ed.). Baltimore, MD: Johns Hopkins University Press.

**Unit 14:**

Karp, H. (2003). *The happiest baby on the block.* New York, NY: Bantam.

Giordano, S. (2006). *The baby sleep solution: a proven program to teach your baby to sleep twelve hours a night.* New York, NY: TarcherPerigee.

Sammons, W. A. H. & Brazelton, T. B. (1991). *The self-calmed baby.* New York, NY: St. Martin's Press.

Hogg, T. (2005). *Secrets of the baby whisperer: how to calm, connect, and communicate with your baby.* New York, NY: Ballantine Books.

Weissbluth, M. (2015). *Healthy sleep habits, happy child.* (4th ed.). New York, NY: Ballantine Books.

Mindell, J. A. (2005). *Sleeping through the night: how infants, toddlers, and their parents can get a good night's sleep.* (2nd ed.). New York, NY: William Morrow.

Ferber, R. (2006). *Solve your child's sleep problems.* (2nd ed). New York, NY: Touchstone.

Ezzo, G. & Buckham, R. (2012). *On becoming babywise: giving your infant the gift of nighttime sleep* (2nd ed.). Sisters, OR: Parent-Wise Solutions.

**Unit 15:**

Karp, H. (2003). *The happiest baby on the block.* New York, NY: Bantam.

Hogg, T. (2005). *Secrets of the baby whisperer: how to calm, connect, and communicate with your baby.* New York, NY: Ballantine Books.

St. James-Roberts, I. (2012). *The origins, prevention and treatment of infant crying and sleep problems.* Abingdon-on-Thames, U.K.: Routledge.

7 swaddles (step-by-step instructional videos) http://www.7swaddles.com/all-videos/

**Unit 16:**

Weissbluth, M. (2015). *Healthy sleep habits, happy child.* (4th ed.). New York, NY: Ballantine Books.

Mindell, J. A. (2005). *Sleeping through the night: how infants, toddlers, and their parents can get a good night's sleep.* (2nd ed.). New York, NY: William Morrow.

Karp, H. (2013). *The happiest baby guide to great sleep: simple solutions for kids from birth to 5 years.* New York, NY: William Morrow Paperbacks.

# Bibliography of Recommended Readings

Ferber, R. (2006). *Solve your child's sleep problems.* (2nd ed). New York, NY: Touchstone.

**Unit 20:**

Oscategui, M. (2012). *Green body, green birth.* (n.p.): US ISBN Agency.

Bock, K. (2008). *Healing the new childhood epidemics: autism, ADHD, asthma, and allergies: the groundbreaking program for the 4-A disorders.* New York, NY: Ballantine Books.

Fassa, L. (2008). *Green babies, sage moms: the ultimate guide to raising your organic baby.* New York, NY: Berkley.

# *Photo attributions for all photos used in NCS Foundational Course*

 By Ernest F (Own work) [GFDL (http://www.gnu.org/copyleft/fdl.html) or CC-BY-SA-3.0 (http://creativecommons.org/licenses/by-sa/3.0/)], via Wikimedia Commons

 By Np0x at English Wikipedia [Public domain], via Wikimedia Commons

 https://commons.wikimedia.org/wiki/File:Postpartum_baby3.jpg

 By The original uploader was Raumka at English Wikipedia (Transferred from en.wikipedia to Commons.) [CC0], via Wikimedia Commons

 By Bonnie U. Gruenberg (Own work) [CC BY-SA 3.0 (https://creativecommons.org/licenses/by-sa/3.0)], via Wikimedia Commons

 https://commons.wikimedia.org/wiki/File:Baby_With_Cradle_Cap.jpg

# *Photo attributions for all photos used in NCS Foundational Course*

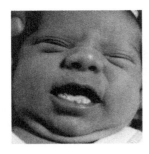

By James Heilman, MD (Own work) [CC BY-SA 3.0 (https://creativecommons.org/licenses/by-sa/3.0) or GFDL (http://www.gnu.org/copyleft/fdl.html)], via Wikimedia Commons

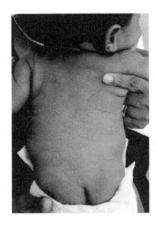

By Gzzz (Own work) [CC BY-SA 4.0 (https://creativecommons.org/licenses/by-sa/4.0)], via Wikimedia Commons

By Bonnie U. Gruenberg (Own work) [CC BY-SA 3.0 (https://creativecommons.org/licenses/by-sa/3.0)], via Wikimedia Commons

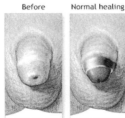

https://medlineplus.gov/ency/presentations/100081_4.htm

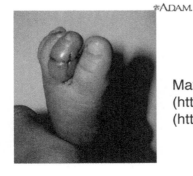

Maxpatrick at the English language Wikipedia [GFDL (http://www.gnu.org/copyleft/fdl.html) or CC-BY-SA-3.0 (http://creativecommons.org/licenses/by-sa/3.0/)], via Wikimedia Commons

# Photo attributions for all photos used in NCS Foundational Course

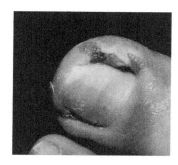

https://commons.wikimedia.org/wiki/File:Toe_(5).JPG

SEXTUPLETS IMAGE: privately owned, used with permission (on file)

http://www.pacifeeder.com

http://podee.com.au

https://www.amazon.com/Bottle-Feeding-Bebe-Sling-LLC/dp/B003Z66XB6

# Photo attributions for all photos used in NCS Foundational Course

http://www.imgrum.org/media/1243699531974726904_2301277836

https://giftshopmag.com/products/oh-baby-showcase/

https://www.amazon.com/BOTTLE-Bottle-Genie-Registry-Feeding/dp/B01KOYWUKO?th=1

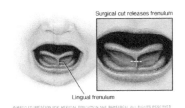

https://www.mayoclinic.org/diseases-conditions/tongue-tie/symptoms-causes/syc-20378452

http://www.tongue-tie-education.com/tie-gallery.html

https://medlineplus.gov/ency/presentations/100095_5.htm

# Photo attributions for all photos used in NCS Foundational Course

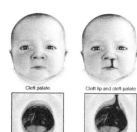

VIDEO:
http://www.nejm.org/doi/full/10.1056/NEJMicm1214572

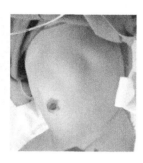

https://www.mayoclinic.org/diseases-conditions/cleft-palate/symptoms-causes/syc-20370985

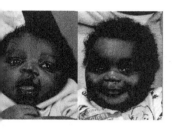

https://www.hopkinsmedicine.org/otolaryngology/specialty_areas/facial_plastic_reconstructive_surgery/reconstructive_procedures/cleft_lip_palate_repair.html

Miracle Blanket VIDEO: https://miraclebabyusa.com/instructions/

# *Photo attributions for all photos used in NCS Foundational Course*

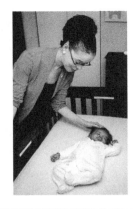

https://www.flickr.com/photos/nichd/18310024960

(NIH flickr account, public domain)

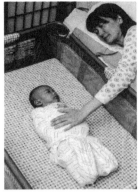

https://www.flickr.com/photos/nichd/17875043184/in/album-72157654071312421/

(NIH flickr account, public domain)

https://www.flickr.com/photos/nichd/18311546989/in/album-72157654071312421/

(NIH flickr account, public domain)

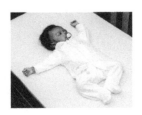

https://www.flickr.com/photos/nichd/17877056223/in/album-72157654071312421/

(NIH flickr account, public domain)

# *Photo attributions for all photos used in NCS Foundational Course*

newborncaresolutions.com

# About the Founder, Tonya Sakowicz

Tonya is an INA Credentialed Nanny, Newborn Care Specialist, CAPPA trained Postpartum Doula and Parent Educator who does both consulting and in-home sleep conditioning and newborn care for her clients as well as the Owner and Director of Education for Newborn Care Solutions, a company dedicated to the specialized training of high-level Newborn Care Specialists and the only company to offer the Master NCS™ training program. Tonya attended Central Washington University, has over 32 years of experience as a Nanny and Newborn Care Specialist and is a proud wife and mother of two children. She is also a certified Eco-Maternity Consultant and Green Birth Educator through her partner company, Baby Go Green.

In addition to be credentialed through the International Nanny Association, Tonya serves as an Officer on the Executive Board, is the past Chair of the Nanny to Nanny Mentoring Program and is currently their NCS Committee chair and in their Monday Mentor Program. Tonya also serves as a Scottsdale Chapter President for DEMA, the Domestic Estate Management Association. Tonya is a highly in-demand speaker for the INA's annual conferences and has spoken at several National Association of Nannies conferences, as well as speaking for APNA, the Association of Premier Nanny Agencies at their annual conference. Tonya has spoken multiple times at National Nanny Training Days around the country and for nanny agencies nationwide. She is a founding member and serves on the advisory board for The Baby Dream Team, a group of dedicated Newborn Care Specialists who offer their services as volunteers to families around the country experiencing the birth of higher order multiples. She is a contributing 'expert' for the website NannyPro.com, has been published in and/or appeared in Parents Magazine, Child Magazine, The Seattle Times, The AZ Republic, The Wall Street Journal and the INA Vision. Tonya has also made numerous television appearances including spots on the news in Seattle, Portland and Phoenix as well as an appearance in 2007 on the Today Show for a special on the Masche Miracles (a family with sextuplets).

Tonya was voted the **Professional Childcare Provider of the Year** in 2003 and nominated for the **International Nanny Association Nanny of the Year** in 2004. In addition, that same year, she was deeply honored with a nomination by her peers for the **National Association of Nannies Harriette Grant Memorial Award**. In 2016, Tonya was honored with the **DEMA Educator of the Year Award** and most recently, in 2017, was again honored with the **DEMA Educator of the Year** and was the recipient of their prestigious **DEMA Lifetime Achievement Award**.

Along with her husband Todd, Tonya has founded Newborn Care Solutions, a company dedicated to education for families with newborns through the training of Newborn Care Specialists and for helping families adjust to life with their newborn baby.

In her spare time, Tonya likes to knit, cook, travel with her family and explore the world underneath the sea through scuba diving around the world.